THE WORD BIRD

Written by
Nicola Davies

Illustrated by
Abbie Cameron

Beak and feather,

Nest and wing

Flap and peck and

hop and sing

They all add up

to just one word...

This book belongs to:

....

....

GRAFFEG

The Word Bird
First published by Graffeg June 2016
© Copyright Graffeg 2016.
This paperback published 2022.

ISBN 9781802584042

Text © 2016 Nicola Davies.
Illustrations © 2016 Abbie Cameron.
Designed and produced by Graffeg
www.graffeg.com

Graffeg Limited, 24 Stradey Park Business
Centre, Mwrwg Road, Llangennech, Llanelli,
Carmarthenshire, SA14 8YP, Wales, UK.
Tel 01554 824000. www.graffeg.com.

FSC
www.fsc.org
MIX
Paper from
responsible sources
FSC® C014138

Yes! It's BIRD!

Teeny tiny, flitting round,

Or huge
and
walking
on the
ground.

Perching high up in a tree,

Or gliding

far, far out at sea.

Hooting in the darkest night,

Or warbling in the dawn's first light.

All so different but just one word describes them all...

That's right, it's BIRD!

Beaks that

sift,

or sew

or grab

And feet that

Paddle,

cling

or stab.

Wings for flapping, soaring, swooping

Or underwater

loop the looping.

with fancy **tails** and **heads** with **crests,**

With plumes and funny blow up chests!

All shapes and colours

but one word
tells us
what

they are...

It's

PUZZLE TO FINISH

And now for a little test...
Can you find each bird its nest?

1

2

3

4

5

A

B

C

D

E

Nicola Davies

Nicola is an award-winning author, whose many books for children include *The Promise* (Green Earth Book Award 2015, CILIP Kate Greenaway Shortlist 2015), *Tiny* (AAAS Subaru Prize 2015), *A First Book of Nature*, *Whale Boy* (Blue Peter Award Shortlist 2014), and the *Heroes of the Wild* series (Portsmouth Book Prize 2014). She graduated in Zoology, studied whales and bats and then worked for the BBC Natural History Unit. Underlying all Nicola's writing is the belief that a relationship with nature is essential to every human being, and that now, more than ever, we need to renew that relationship. Nicola's children's books from Graffeg include *Perfect* (CILIP Kate Greenaway Longlist 2017), *The Pond* (CILIP Kate Greenaway Longlist 2018), *The New Girl* and the Shadows and Light, Country Tales and Animal Surprises series.

Abbie Cameron

Abbie Cameron was raised on the farmlands of the West Country. Surrounded by nature, she developed a love and appreciation for all creatures great and small. Abbie studied Illustration at University of Wales Trinity Saint David, where she first met Nicola Davies. Her style is playful and inventive, sharing some of the tongue-in-cheek attitude and doodle-like style of other contemporary British illustrators. She employs the use of bright colours and texture whilst playing with scale, composition and open space. Abbie's other books include *Animal Surprises* (The Klaus Flugge Prize for the Most Exciting Newcomer to Picture Book Illustration Longlist 2017), *The Word Bird* and *Into the Blue*, as well as their companion series of How to Draw books. Abbie was also highly commended in the Penguin Random House Design Awards 2014.

Rhyming Book Series

Discover the delights of nature with zoologist and top children's author Nicola Davies. Follow the young adventurer as she treks through the jungle in Animal Surprises, dives deep down into the sea in *Into the Blue*, climbs up high into the trees in *The Word Bird* , discovers the wonders hidden inside eggs of all shapes and sizes in *The Secret of the Egg* and journeys around the world to uncover the world of spiders, mini-beasts and more in *Invertebrates are Cool!*. Each rhyming book is fully illustrated in colour by Abbie Cameron.

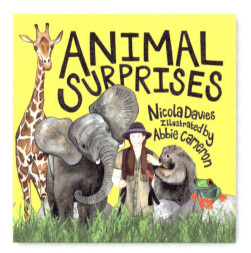

Animal Surprises
ISBN 9781910862445

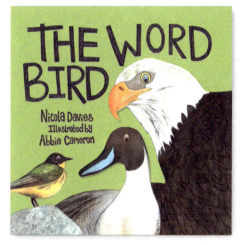

The Word Bird
ISBN 9781910862438

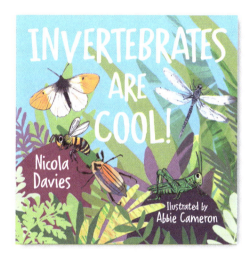

Invertebrates are Cool!
ISBN 9781912213696

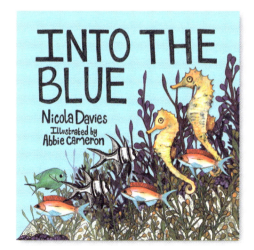

Into the Blue
ISBN 9781910862452

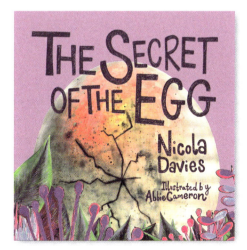

The Secret of the Egg
ISBN 9781912213672

www.graffeg.com

How to Draw Series

In this companion series, Abbie Cameron teaches children how to draw their favourite animals from the rhyming books step-by-step, alongside informative text about each species from Nicola Davies.

Titles in the series:

• Animal Surprises: How to Draw
• The Word Bird: How to Draw
• Into the Blue: How to Draw

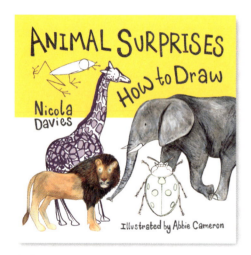

Animal Surprises: How to Draw
ISBN 9781912050567

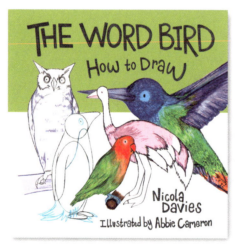

The Word Bird: How to Draw
ISBN 9781912050574

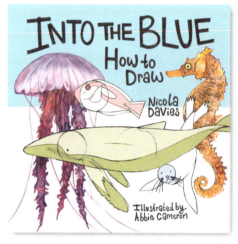

Into the Blue: How to Draw
ISBN 9781912050550

Visit **graffeg.com/pages/how-to-draw** to watch Abbie drawing some of the animals from the series with step-by-step instructions.

www.graffeg.com